CONTENTS

¡BIENVENIDO A PUERTO RICO! 4
WILD PUERTO RICO 8
HUMANS ARRIVE 12
PUERTO RICO GETS ITS NAME 14
SPANISH RULE 16
THE UNITED STATES TAKES OVER 20
HURRICANE DISASTER 24
PUERTO RICO TODAY AND TOMORROW 26
TIMELINE 29
GLOSSARY 30
FOR MORE INFORMATION 31
INDEX 32

¡Bienvenido a Puerto Rico!

¡Bienvenido a Puerto Rico! That's Spanish for "Welcome to Puerto Rico!" Spain ruled Puerto Rico for centuries, and Spanish remains—along with English—an official language of this U.S. territory.

Puerto Rico is between the northeast Caribbean Sea and the Atlantic Ocean. It's about 1,000 miles (1,609 km) southeast of Florida. People often think of Puerto Rico as a single island, but it's actually an archipelago, or group of islands. Most people live on the main island—the largest island—and only two of the smaller islands are occupied year-round.

The main island is about 111 miles (179 km) east to west and 39 miles (63 km) north to south. It's nearly twice the size of Delaware, one of the smallest U.S. states.

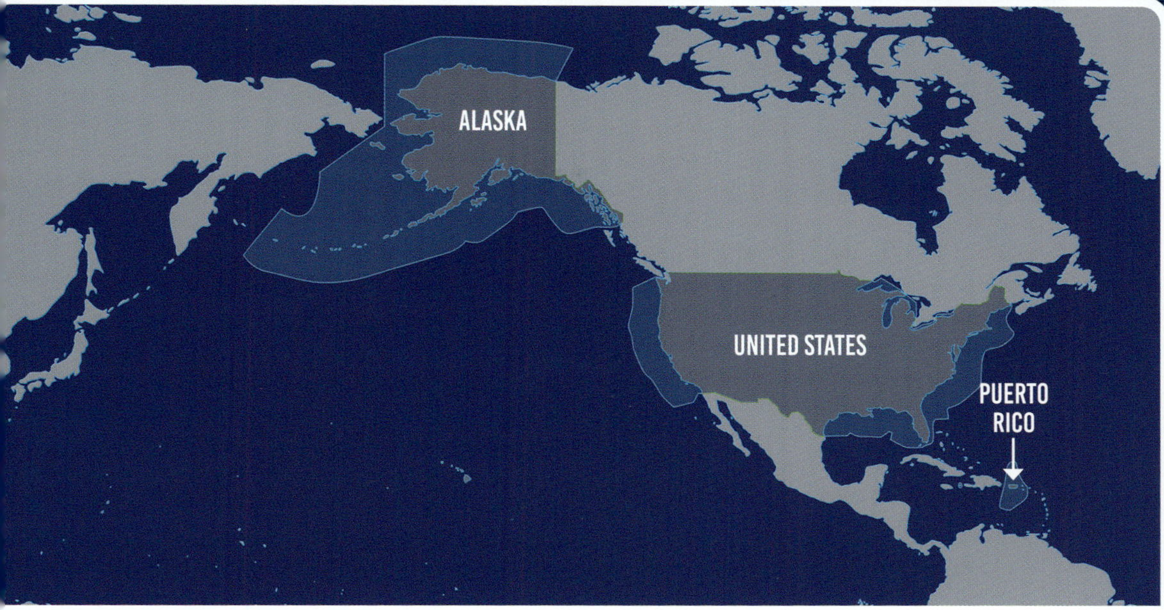

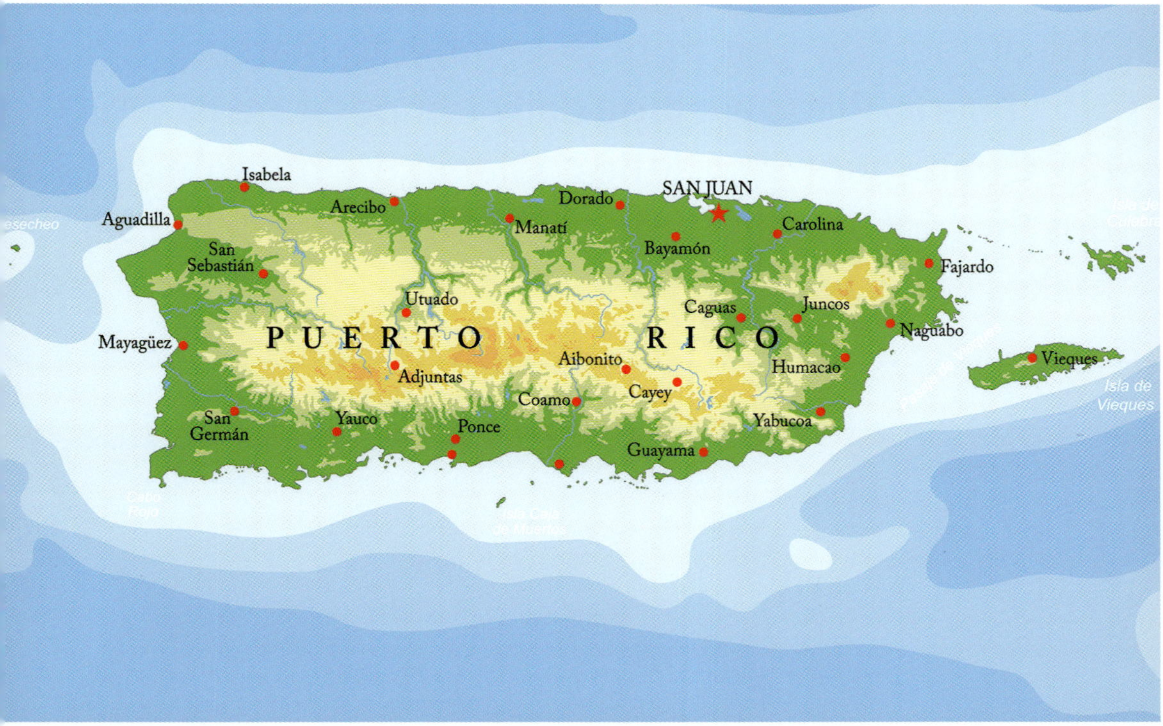

Puerto Rico is the name for both the archipelago and the main island. In this book, we'll use the name Puerto Rico to indicate the main island.

Lowlands lie along Puerto Rico's coasts, but mountains and hills cover most of the land. The central mountain range, called the Cordillera Central, runs from west to east. The highest point is Cerro de Punta, which is 4,390 feet (1,338 m) tall.

Puerto Rico is in the **tropics**, and that location determines its climate. Unlike many parts of the U.S. mainland, Puerto Rico doesn't have four seasons—it has only two: a rainy season and a dry season. The rainy season generally lasts from April to November. The dry season runs from December to March.

Puerto Rico's average daily temperature is 79°F (26°C), although it's a little cooler in the mountains. But the high humidity, or level of moisture in the air, makes it feel warmer.

Territorial Truths ☆☆☆☆☆

The Puerto Rico Trench, the deepest place in the Atlantic Ocean, lies near Puerto Rico. At its deepest point, it reaches down 27,559 feet (8,400 m). That's more than 5 miles (8 km)!

Territories of the United States

PUERTO RICO

Janey Levy

PowerKiDS press

Published in 2025 by The Rosen Publishing Group, Inc.
2544 Clinton Street, Buffalo, NY 14224

First Edition

Editor: Therese Shea
Book Design: Rachel Rising

Photo Credits: Cover, Darryl Brooks/Shutterstock.com; Cover, pp. 1, 3–32 boromvit tatasai/Shutterstock.com; Cover, pp. 1, 3–32 P-fotography/Shutterstock.com; Cover, pp. 1, 7, 9, 11, 13, 17, 19, 21, 23, 25, 27, 29 https://commons.wikimedia.org/wiki/File:Flag_of_Puerto_Rico.svg; p. 4 zmotions/Shutterstock.com; p. 5 Rainer Lesniewski/Shutterstock.com; p. 5 (bottom) Serban Bogdan/Shutterstock.com; pp. 7, 9 Dennis van de Water/Shutterstock.com; p. 9 (bird) Vinicius R. Souza/Shutterstock.com; p. 11 Photo Spirit/Shutterstock.com; p. 13 https://en.m.wikipedia.org/wiki/File:Ta%C3%ADno_women_preparing_cassava_bread.png; p. 14 balabolka/Shutterstock.com; p. 15 Darryl Brooks/Shuttestock.com; p. 17 Songquan Deng/Shutterstock.com; p. 19 Venturelli Luca/Shutterstock.com; p. 21 https://commons.wikimedia.org/wiki/File:John_Hay_signs_Treaty_of_Paris,_1899.JPG; p. 23 https://commons.wikimedia.org/wiki/File:HarryTruman.jpg; p. 25 https://en.m.wikipedia.org/wiki/File:20171007-_SC_National_Guard_in_Puerto_Rico_(36846539124).jpg; p. 27 Glynnis Jones/Shutterstock.com.

Library of Congress Cataloging-in-Publication Data

Names: Levy, Janey, author.
Title: Puerto Rico / Janey Levy.
Description: Buffalo, New York : PowerKids Press, [2025] | Series: Territories of the United States | Includes bibliographical references and index.
Identifiers: LCCN 2024002584 (print) | LCCN 2024002585 (ebook) | ISBN 9781725329157 (library binding) | ISBN 9781725329133 (paperback) | ISBN 9781725329164 (ebook)
Subjects: LCSH: Puerto Rico--History--Juvenile literature. | Natural history--Puerto Rico--Juvenile literature.
Classification: LCC F1958.3 .L47 2025 (print) | LCC F1958.3 (ebook) | DDC 972.95--dc23/eng/20240213
LC record available at https://lccn.loc.gov/2024002584
LC ebook record available at https://lccn.loc.gov/2024002585

Manufactured in the United States of America

CPSIA Compliance Information: Batch #CSPK25. For further information contact Rosen Publishing at 1-800-237-9932.

MAGNIFICENT UNDERGROUND RIVERS AND CAVES

Puerto Rico is home to the third-largest cave system in the world and the largest in the **Western Hemisphere**. Cavernas del Río Camuy is in the northern part of the island and was carved by the Río Camuy (Camuy River) as the river ran underground. The cave system contains over 220 caves covering 286 acres (116 ha). The largest cave—Cueva Clara—soars high enough that a 20-story building could fit inside!

This shows narrow lowlands along the coast, with the hills rising behind them.

Wild Puerto Rico

Puerto Rico's tropical climate makes it a perfect home for a rich variety of plants and animals. One of the most spectacular areas is the El Yunque rainforest, in the Luquillo Mountains in eastern Puerto Rico.

El Yunque has over 240 species of trees. Of those, 88 species are rare, and 23 are found only in this rainforest. El Yunque also contains 50 species of orchids, over 150 species of **ferns**, and many species of vines and mosses.

Although no large animals live in the rainforest, it's home to 11 species of bats and 8 species of lizards, as well as nonpoisonous snakes, mongooses, insects, and **rodents**. More than 95 species of birds live there, including the **endangered** Puerto Rican parrot.

Territorial Truths ☆☆☆☆☆

One common animal found in El Yunque is a tiny frog called the coquí. It gets its name from the male's nighttime call: KOH-KEE. It's become a kind of symbol of Puerto Rican **culture**.

AMAZONA VITTATA, THE PUERTO RICAN PARROT

Scientists believe Puerto Rican parrots have lived in the territory for over 1,000 years. At one time, up to 1 million parrots may have lived on the island. But over the centuries, people cut down the forest to use the land for agriculture. This destroyed the parrot's habitat, the place that provided everything it needed to live and flourish. Today, about 250 Puerto Rican parrots live in the wild on the island.

Rainforests get their name from the fact that they get lots of rain. It rains four times a day in El Yunque, adding up to 200 inches (506 cm) of rain annually. That equals over 100 billion gallons (379 billion L) of water!

Southwestern Puerto Rico has a region that's El Yunque's complete opposite. It's the Guánica Biosphere Reserve and State Forest. This dry region gets only about 30 inches (76 cm) of rainfall a year.

The over 700 plant species here cover an amazing range. You can find deciduous trees—trees that shed their leaves—evergreen trees, and even cactus. Among these are 48 endangered plants—such as the sebucan cactus—and 16 that are native to the region, such as the guayacán tree.

A rich variety of animals lives here, including the coquí frog and at least 185 bird species. Several endangered animals make their homes here, including a bird called the Puerto Rican nightjar, the Puerto Rican crested toad, and the red land crab.

Territorial Truths ☆☆☆☆☆

At least 16 species of birds are endemic to Puerto Rico, and many of them can be found in Guánica. These include both the Puerto Rican woodpecker and the endangered Puerto Rican nightjar.

GUÁNICA'S COASTAL AREAS

There's more to Guánica in the surrounding ocean. Mangroves grow along the coast. These are tropical trees adapted to live in salt water and loose, wet soils and can stand to be covered by tides. The waters are home to many coral, animal, and plant species, including the West Indian manatee. Manatees are large, grayish marine mammals with a heavy, wrinkled head with whiskers; two flippers; and a paddle-shaped tail. They eat seaweed in Guánica's underwater prairies.

One of the most famous plants in Guánica is a guayacán tree, which may be 1,000 years old! A guayacán tree is shown here.

Humans Arrive

Little is known about Puerto Rico's most ancient people, the Archaics, who arrived almost 6,000 years ago. Scientists believe they came from the coast of what's now Venezuela in South America.

Around 300 CE, the Arawak Indians—also from what's now Venezuela—arrived. And by 1000 CE, Taíno (tah-EE-noh, or TY-noh) culture had developed. These were the people who greeted Christopher Columbus in 1493.

The Taíno lived in small villages led by a cacique, or chief. Their homes were built of logs and poles and covered with thatched roofs. They hunted small animals and caught seafood. They grew crops such as pineapples, corn, sweet potatoes, beans, squash, tobacco, and peanuts. The Taíno painted themselves on special occasions and wore jewelry that was sometimes made of gold.

Territorial Truths ☆☆☆☆☆

It's likely you've used Taíno words. The Taíno invented many words we commonly use, such as canoe, barbecue, tobacco, hurricane, potato, and corn.

MORE ABOUT THE TAÍNO

Christopher Columbus recorded his impressions of the Taíno. He wrote: "They traded with us and gave us everything they had, with good will . . . They are very gentle and without knowledge of what is evil; nor do they murder or steal . . . They love their neighbors as themselves, and they have the sweetest talk in the world, and are gentle and always laughing."

The Taíno name for Puerto Rico was Borikén (or Borinquén or Boriquén), which means "land of the brave lord." They called themselves Boricua, a name still used today.

Puerto Rico Gets Its Name

How did the island's name switch from Borikén to Puerto Rico? The change started with Christopher Columbus's arrival in 1493.

Columbus claimed the island for Spain and named it San Juan Bautista, after the Christian figure Saint John the Baptist. In 1508, Spanish explorer Juan Ponce de León established the first European settlement, named Caparra, near a bay on the island's north shore. Because of the valuable mining being done there, the town was renamed Puerto Rico, or "rich port," in 1521.

But over time, people began to use the name Puerto Rico for the whole island and the name San Juan for the port. And that's how it is today: the island is Puerto Rico, and the city is San Juan.

San Juan has been the capital of Puerto Rico since the Spanish founded it. Today, its population is about 335,000.

Spanish Rule

Although Columbus claimed Puerto Rico for Spain in 1493, Spain neglected the island until 1508. That's when Spanish officials authorized Ponce de León to explore and conquer it.

The Taíno welcomed Ponce de León at first. But conflicts soon broke out as the Spanish forced the Taíno to submit to Spanish control. The Spanish then enslaved the Taíno. Within a year, Ponce de León had conquered most of the island and its people.

The Taíno suffered terribly. They were forced to work in the gold mines under awful conditions. Many died from the hard labor. Many more died from diseases the Spanish brought because the Taíno had no immunity to them. The desperate Taíno revolted against the Spanish beginning in 1511. But the Spanish, with better weapons, easily defeated the Taíno.

Territorial Truths

Slavery and European diseases destroyed the Taíno. Experts estimate 30,000 to 50,000 Taíno lived in Puerto Rico when Columbus arrived. By 1514, only about 4,000 remained, and by 1530, there were only about 1,150.

WHO WAS JUAN PONCE DE LEÓN?

Juan Ponce de León was born around 1460 to a Spanish noble family. He joined Columbus's 1493 expedition and wound up on **Hispaniola** in 1502. But rumors of gold drew him to Puerto Rico in 1508. He soon became governor there, but political enemies forced him out. He later wound up in Florida while searching for the island of Bimini. He died in 1521 after being wounded by a Native American attack in Florida.

Ponce de León was one of the Spanish conquistadors in the Americas. The conquistadors were Spanish explorers and conquerors searching for wealth, power, and new trading opportunities.

Because so many Taíno had died, the Spanish needed more workers for the gold mines. In 1513, they began to use enslaved Africans and **Indigenous** peoples from nearby islands. But the island was stripped of its gold by 1540, causing many European settlers to leave Puerto Rico. Those who remained found other ways to profit. They used the enslaved people to grow and harvest crops such as **sugarcane**, ginger, tobacco, and coffee.

The Spanish on Puerto Rico faced some challenges. Puerto Rico's wealth and location made it a target for Spain's enemies. Caribs, who were native to nearby islands, pirates, and other European countries attacked Puerto Rico. So, the Spanish built fortresses and surrounded San Juan with a massive wall to fight off attacks. But Spain couldn't hold Puerto Rico forever.

Territorial Truths ☆☆☆☆☆

In 1868, about 600 people in the mountain town of Lares revolted against their Spanish rulers. The Spanish easily triumphed, but the uprising became a symbol of Puerto Rico's struggle for independence.

ROBERTO COFRESÍ, PUERTO RICAN PIRATE

Do you know the tale of Robin Hood, the British thief who robbed the rich and gave to the poor? Puerto Rico had its own Robin Hood—a pirate named Roberto Cofresí. He was born in 1791 in a small seaside town called Cabo Rojo. From there, he attacked the ships of Spain's enemies. He shared the wealth he stole with people in need, so the people protected him. But he was finally captured and put to death in 1825.

You can still see parts of the stone wall the Spanish built around San Juan in the early 1600s. It was 25 feet (8 m) high and 18 feet (5 m) thick!

The United States Takes Over

Spain controlled Puerto Rico until 1898, when the Spanish-American War broke out in Cuba. It wasn't a long-fought war because Spain lacked the power it once had. The war began in April 1898, and fighting ended four months later. The war officially ended in December 1898 with the Treaty of Paris. In the treaty, Spain handed control of Puerto Rico to the United States.

The United States appointed a military governor to rule the island. The military government established a public school system, managed government finances, and constructed public works such as highways and **sanitation** systems. But problems resulted because the U.S. government didn't understand Puerto Rican culture and politics. In 1900, a law called the Foraker Act established a civilian, or nonmilitary, government on the island.

Territorial Truths ☆☆☆☆☆

Members of Puerto Rico's Nationalist Party were willing to fight for independence. Two nationalists tried to kill President Harry Truman in 1950. In 1954, four nationalists fired weapons in the U.S. House of Representatives, wounding five congressmen.

PUERTO RICO'S POLITICAL STATUS

Ever since the United States took control of Puerto Rico in 1898, the island's leaders have tried to modify its political relationship with the United States. Some leaders wanted the island to become a U.S. state. Others simply wanted Puerto Rico to have more autonomy, or control over its own affairs. Then, in the 1920s, the Nationalist Party arose. It favored independence—immediate independence—for Puerto Rico. Puerto Ricans continue to have mixed ideas about the future political status of their homeland.

Here, U.S. Secretary of State John Hay signs an official paper after Congress approved the Treaty of Paris in 1899.

Under the Foraker Act, the United States controlled Puerto Rican affairs. Puerto Ricans resented this situation. For the last year of Spanish rule, Puerto Ricans had enjoyed much more autonomy, and they wanted that again.

The United States has been slow to grant Puerto Rico autonomy. In 1917, Puerto Ricans were granted U.S. citizenship. In 1948, they elected their own governor for the first time. Then, in 1952, Puerto Rico became a U.S. commonwealth. Puerto Ricans could now create their own constitution and control some local matters, including elections, taxes, education, health care, and housing. But Congress and the president still control matters such as citizenship, defense, **currency**, and trade. And Congress or the president can veto, or reject, decisions of the island's legislature.

Territorial Truths ☆☆☆☆☆

Puerto Ricans have voted six times on whether the island should remain a commonwealth, become a state, or become independent. In 2012 and 2020, they voted in favor of becoming a state.

BEING A U.S. CITIZEN IN PUERTO RICO

You might imagine that, as U.S. citizens, Puerto Ricans have the same rights as other U.S. citizens. But that's not true. The island's people can't vote for president—and that's an important right! They can elect a representative to the U.S. House of Representatives. But that person can only vote on matters within the committees they serve on. They can't vote on matters brought before the whole House, such as the passage of U.S. laws.

President Harry Truman signed the law that made Puerto Rico a U.S. commonwealth.

Hurricane Disaster

Although Puerto Rico's tropical location sounds lovely, it puts the island in danger from one of nature's most destructive forces: hurricanes.

The recording of hurricanes began in 1508, when the Spanish arrived. Over 120 have hit Puerto Rico since then. But we know earlier hurricanes struck the island; the Taíno invented the word hurricane!

Puerto Rico suffered terrible hurricane damage in 2017. On September 6, Hurricane Irma's winds and rain hit the island. Then, on September 20, the extremely powerful Hurricane Maria struck. Its winds reached 155 miles (250 km) per hour. Parts of Puerto Rico received 30 inches (76 cm) of rain in a single day. The storm caused flooding; destroyed trees, buildings, and roads; and knocked out power and communications. Almost 3,000 people died. Puerto Rico is still recovering.

Territorial Truths ☆☆☆☆☆

Hurricane Fiona struck Puerto Rico on September 18, 2022. It wasn't as strong as Hurricane Maria, but it still caused flooding and landslides and knocked out the island's electricity.

PUERTO RICO'S WORST HURRICANE

As terrible as Hurricane Maria was, Puerto Rico suffered through an even worse one on August 8, 1899: Hurricane San Ciriaco. Its winds reached an estimated 145 miles (233 km) per hour. In two days, the island received about two months' worth of rain. The hurricane destroyed about 250,000 homes and nearly all crops. Most people had no way to get food or clean water. Almost 3,400 people died.

The damage from Hurricane Maria was estimated to be more than $90 billion.

Puerto Rico Today and Tomorrow

Today, Puerto Rico is home to about 3.2 million people. Its vibrant culture reflects the island's history. It blends Taíno, Spanish, and African traditions, food, music, dance, art, literature, and language. There are also influences from U.S. mainland culture and from Chinese and European people who have moved to the island.

However, Puerto Rico and its people face serious financial problems. The island prospered financially in the late 20th century, partly because of a 1976 U.S. tax law. U.S. companies could build factories in Puerto Rico and not pay taxes on their earnings there. So, manufacturing and jobs flourished. But the law changed in 1996, and manufacturing and jobs dropped. Puerto Rico's government started borrowing money to keep up with spending. But by 2015, Puerto Rico couldn't pay its debts, or bills.

Territorial Truths ☆☆☆☆☆

Tourists play a major part in Puerto Rico's economy today. More than 2 million people visit each year, and over 91,500 Puerto Ricans work in the tourism industry.

FAMOUS PUERTO RICANS

Puerto Rico's rich culture has produced many people whose names you might recognize. Rita Moreno, Benicio del Toro, Joaquin Phoenix, and Luis Guzmán are famous Puerto Rican actors. Famous musicians include Ricky Martin, Daddy Yankee, Chayanne, José Feliciano, and Bad Bunny. Among the famous athletes are Roberto Clemente, Héctor "Macho" Camacho, Juan "Chi-Chi" Rodríguez, and Mónica Puig. And Vanessa Aponte Williams and Miguel Morales are leading scientists. These Puerto Ricans and others have made enormous contributions to world culture.

Puerto Ricans have protested to bring the issues of the island to the attention of mainland Americans.

Costly natural **disasters** have added to Puerto Rico's problems. You've read about the island's hurricane problems. Puerto Rico also experiences earthquakes. On average, five strike every month! And the COVID-19 **pandemic** added to Puerto Rico's troubles, beginning in 2020. It caused the government to impose restrictions, or limits, that harmed the important tourism industry.

Experts say the island's government made problems worse by not making good use of the money it borrowed. Roads, electricity, health care, and the education system are still in need of repair.

So, what now? In 2022, the territorial government and the federal government agreed on a plan to reduce the island's debt and help it pay back what it owes. But critics say the plan doesn't address many problems. Only the future will show if Puerto Rico's situation improves.

Territorial Truths ☆☆☆☆☆

The beginning of 2020 saw Puerto Rico rattled by over 400 earthquakes in three weeks. And over 9,400 earthquakes struck that year.

TIMELINE

ABOUT 4000 BCE	The first people arrive in Puerto Rico, likely from Venezuela.
ABOUT 300 CE	The Arawak people from Venezuela arrive.
ABOUT 1000 CE	Taíno culture flourishes.
1493	Christopher Columbus lands on Puerto Rico and claims it for Spain.
1508	Juan Ponce de León establishes the first Spanish settlement on Puerto Rico.
1898	The United States wins the Spanish-American War and takes control of Puerto Rico
1917	Puerto Ricans are granted U.S. citizenship.
1952	Puerto Rico gains commonwealth status and creates its own constitution.
2012	Puerto Ricans vote for U.S. statehood for the first time.
2015	Economic crisis forces Puerto Rico to announce it can't pay its debts.
2017	Hurricane Maria causes enormous destruction.
2020	Puerto Rico experiences terrible earthquake damage.

Glossary

culture: The beliefs and ways of life of a group of people.

currency: A kind of money that a country uses.

disaster: An event that causes much suffering or loss.

endangered: In danger of dying out.

fern: A type of flowerless plant with leaves called fronds.

Hispaniola: The island that today includes Haiti and the Dominican Republic.

indigenous: Having to do with the earliest known people of a place.

pandemic: A time or event in which a disease spreads quickly and affects a large number of people in a wide area or around the world.

rodent: A small, furry animal with large front teeth, such as a mouse or rat.

sanitation: Having to do with actions taken for health and cleanliness.

sugarcane: A tall grass grown in warm places as a source of sugar.

tropics: The part of Earth that's near the equator and has very warm weather.

Western Hemisphere: A hemisphere is one-half of Earth. The Western Hemisphere is the half that contains North and South America.

For More Information

Books

Goldsworthy, Steve. *Puerto Rico*. New York, NY: Lightbox Learning, 2023.

Klepeis, Alicia. *Puerto Rico*. Minneapolis, MN: Bellwether Media, 2022.

Sebra, Richard. *Puerto Rico*. Minneapolis, MN: Core Library, 2023.

Websites

Britannica Kids: Puerto Rico
kids.britannica.com/students/article/Puerto-Rico/276577
Learn all about Puerto Rico, its people, land, culture, plants, animals, and history.

Facts About Puerto Rico
www.kids-world-travel-guide.com/facts-about-puerto-rico.html
Discover more fascinating facts about this U.S. territory.

National Geographic Kids: Puerto Rico
kids.nationalgeographic.com/geography/states/article/puerto-rico
See some great pictures of Puerto Rico on this website.

INDEX

A
Africa, 18, 26
agriculture, 9, 12, 18
Arawak Indians, 12
Archaics, 12
Atlantic Ocean, 4, 6, 11

C
Caribbean Sea, 4
Caribs, 18
Cavernas del Río Camuy, 7
Cerro de Punta, 6
citizenship, 22, 23
climate/weather, 6, 8, 9, 10, 24, 25, 28
Cofresí, Roberto, 19
Columbus, Christopher, 12, 13, 14, 16, 17
Congress (U.S.), 20, 21, 22, 23
Cordillera Central, 6
COVID-19, 28
Cueva Clara, 7

E
earthquake, 28
El Yunque rainforest, 8, 9, 10
enslavement, 16, 18

F
fishing, 12
Foraker Act, 20, 22

G
Guánica Biosphere Reserve and State Forest, 10, 11

H
Hay, John, 21
hunting, 12

I
independence, 18, 20, 21

J
John the Baptist, Saint, 14

L
language, 4
lowlands, 6
Luquillo Mountains, 8

M
mining, 14, 16, 18
mountains, 6, 8, 18

N
Nationalist Party, 20, 21

P
pirates, 18
plants, 8, 10
Ponce de León, Juan, 14, 16, 17
Puerto Rico Trench, 6

R
rainforest, 8, 9
Río Camuy, 7

S
San Juan, 14, 15, 19
Spain, 4, 16, 17, 18, 20, 22, 24, 26
Spanish-American War, 20

T
Taíno people, 12, 13, 16, 18, 24, 26
tourism, 26
Treaty of Paris, 20, 21
Truman, Harry, 20, 23

U
United States, 20, 21, 22, 23

V
Venezuela, 12
voting, 22, 23

W
wildlife, 8, 9, 10, 11